HAL LEONARD

GUITAR METHOD BOOK 1
LEFT-HANDED EDITION

BY WILL SCHMID AND GREG KOCH

ISBN 978-1-4234-8440-0

HAL•LEONARD®
CORPORATION
7777 W. BLUEMOUND RD. P.O. BOX 13819 MILWAUKEE, WI 53213

T0057677

Visit Hal Leonard Online at
www.halleonard.com

YOUR GUITAR

This book is designed for use with any type of guitar—acoustic steel-string, nylon-string classical, or electric. Any of these guitars can be adapted for use in a wide variety of styles of music.

STEEL-STRING

NYLON-STRING

ELECTRIC

If you are using a solidbody-electric or an acoustic-electric be sure to practice with an amplifier some of the time.

TUNING

Tuning Keys

When you are tuning your guitar, you will adjust the pitch (highness or lowness of sound) of each string by turning the corresponding tuning key. Tightening a string raises the pitch and loosening it lowers the pitch.

The strings are numbered 1 through 6 beginning with the thinnest string, the one closest to your knee. Follow the instructions below to tune each string in sequence, beginning with the sixth string.

TUNING WITH AN ELECTRONIC TUNER

An electronic tuner "reads" the pitch of a sound and tells you whether or not the pitch is correct. Until your ear is well trained in hearing pitches, this can be a much more accurate way to tune. There are many different types of tuners available, and each one will come with more detailed instructions for its use.

TUNING TO A KEYBOARD

If you have a piano or electric keyboard nearby, play the correct key (see diagram) and slowly turn the corresponding tuning key until the sound of the string matches the sound of the keyboard.

ANOTHER WAY TO TUNE

To check or correct your tuning when no pitch source is available, follow these steps:
- Assume that the sixth string is tuned correctly to E.
- Press the sixth string at the 5th fret. This is the pitch A to which you tune your open fifth string. Play the depressed sixth string and the fifth string with your thumb. When the two sounds match, you are in tune.
- Press the fifth string at the 5th fret and tune the open fourth string to it. Follow the same procedure that you did on the fifth and sixth strings.
- Press the fourth string at the 5th fret and tune the open third string to it.
- To tune the second string, press the third string at the 4th fret and tune the open second string to it.
- Press the second string at the 5th fret and tune the first string to it.

This is called **relative tuning** because the strings are tuned relative to one another.

PLAYING POSITION

There are several ways to hold the guitar comfortably. On the left is a typical seated position, and on the right is the standing position. Make sure you practice sitting and standing. Observe the following general guidelines in forming your playing posture:

- Position your body, arms, and legs in such a way that you avoid tension.

- If you feel tension creeping into your playing, you probably need to reassess your position.

- Tilt the neck upwards—never down.

- Keep the body of the guitar as vertical as possible. Avoid slanting the top of the guitar so that you can see better. Balance your weight evenly from left to right. Sit straight (but not rigid).

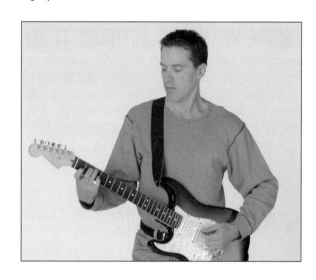

Right-hand fingers are numbered 1 through 4 (Pianists: Note that the thumb is not number 1.) Place the thumb in back of the neck roughly opposite the 2nd finger. Avoid gripping the neck like a baseball bat with the palm touching the back of the neck.

These photos show the position for holding a pick and the right-hand position in relationship to the strings. Strive for finger efficiency and relaxation in your playing.

MUSICAL SYMBOLS

Music is written in **notes** on a **staff**. The staff has five lines and four spaces between the lines. Where a note is written on the staff determines its **pitch** (highness or lowness). At the beginning of the staff is a **clef sign**. Guitar music is written in the treble clef.

STAFF

TREBLE CLEF

Each line and space of the staff has a letter name. The **lines** are, (from bottom to top) E - G - B - D - F, which you can remember as Every Guitarist Begins Doing Fine. The **spaces** are, (from bottom to top) F - A - C - E, which spells "Face."

LINES

E G B D F

SPACES

F A C E

The staff is divided into several parts by bar lines. The space between two bar lines is called a **measure** (also known as a "bar"). To end a piece of music a double bar is placed on the staff.

MEASURE

BAR LINES

BAR LINE   BAR LINE   DOUBLE BAR

Each measure contains a group of **beats**. Beats are the steady pulse of music. You respond to the pulse or beat when you tap your foot.

The two numbers placed next to the clef sign are the time signature.
The top number tells you how many beats are in one measure.

TIME SIGNATURE

FOUR BEATS PER MEASURE
QUARTER NOTE (♩) GETS ONE BEAT

The bottom number of the time signature tells you what kind of note will receive one beat.

Notes indicate the length (number of counts) of musical sound.

NOTES

WHOLE NOTE = 4 beats   HALF NOTE = 2 beats   QUARTER NOTE = 1 beat

When different kinds of notes are placed on different lines or spaces, you will know the pitch of the note and how long to play the sound.

NOTES ON THE FIRST STRING

E   F   G

OPEN   1st FRET   3rd FRET
           1st FINGER 3rd FINGER

E   F   G

This sign (⊓) tells you to strike the string with a downward motion of the pick.

1 COUNT: 1 - 2 - 3 - 4   1 - 2 - 3 - 4   1 - 2 - 3 - 4   1 - 2 - 3 - 4   1 - 2 - 3 - 4

Hold down 1st finger

2 1 - 2   3 - 4   1 - 2   3 - 4   1 - 2   3 - 4   1 - 2   3 - 4   1 - 2 - 3 - 4

3 1   2   3   4   1   2   3   4   1   2   3   4   1   2   3 - 4

At first practice the exercises slowly and steadily. When you can play them well at a slow speed, gradually increase the tempo (speed).

Touch only the tips of the fingers on the strings.

Keep the right hand fingers arched over the strings.

Some songs are longer than one line. When you reach the end of the first line of music, continue on to the second line without stopping. Gray letters above the staff indicate chords to be played by your teacher. Measure numbers are given at the beginning of each new line of music.

SPANISH THEME

7

NOTES ON THE SECOND STRING

B   C   D

OPEN

OPEN   1st FRET / 1st FINGER   3rd FRET / 3rd FINGER

B   C   D

9

Hold down 1st finger _

COUNT: 1 - 2 - 3 - 4   1 - 2 - 3 - 4   1 - 2 - 3 - 4   1 - 2 - 3 - 4   1 - 2 - 3 - 4

10

1 - 2   3 - 4   1 - 2   3 - 4   1 - 2   3 - 4   1 - 2   3 - 4   1 - 2 - 3 - 4

11

1   2   3   4   1   2   3   4   1   2   3   4   1   2   3   4   1 - 2 - 3 - 4

Always practice the exercises slowly and steadily at first. After you can play them well at a slower tempo, gradually increase the speed. If some of your notes are fuzzy or unclear, move your right-hand finger slightly until you get a clear sound.

12

13

MOVING FROM STRING TO STRING

You have learned six notes now, three on the first string and three on the second string. In the following exercises you will be moving from string to string. As you are playing one note, look ahead to the next and get your fingers in position.

14

STRING: ② ①
FINGER: open   1st   3rd   open   1st   3rd

15

WORLD BEAT

16

Practice these songs played on strings 1 and 2. Always begin slowly and then gradually increase the tempo. Gray chord symbols are used throughout the book to indicate that the chords should be played by the instructor.

ODE TO JOY

Beethoven

BLUES

NOTES ON THE THIRD STRING

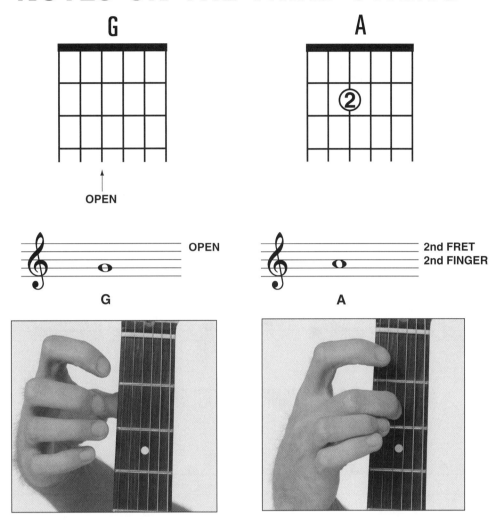

G   A

OPEN

OPEN   G

2nd FRET
2nd FINGER   A

Keep the fingers arched over the strings at all times so they will be in position to finger the next note.

19

20

THREE-STRING REVIEW

Here are all the notes we've learned so far.

G A B C D E F G

E B G
F C
A
G D

Play through these notes up and down. Then play just the. low G and the high G, and notice how similar they sound.
The distance between two different notes with the same letter name is called an **octave**.

The following songs use notes on strings 1, 2, and 3.

A **duet** is a song that has two parts that can be played together. Practice both parts of the following duet. Ask your instructor or a friend to play the duet with you.

AU CLAIR DE LA LUNE

France

PRACTICE TIP

Regular practice is essential. Practicing a half hour each day is better than practicing two hours every four days. Find a regular time of the day that works for you.

AURA LEE

Poulton/Fosdick

3/4 TIME

Some music has three beats per measure instead of four. This is indicated by the top number of the time signature. The bottom number (4) tells you that the quarter note gets one beat.

A dot after a note increases its value by one-half. In $\frac{3}{4}$ time a dotted half note (𝅗𝅥.) gets three beats.

THREE BEATS PER MEASURE
QUARTER NOTE (♩)
GETS ONE BEAT

$$\frac{3}{4} \quad \text{𝅗𝅥} \; + \; \text{.} \; = \; \text{𝅗𝅥.}$$

2 beats   1 beat   3 beats

COUNT: 1   2   3   1 - 2   3   1   2   3   1 - 2 - 3   1   2 - 3   1 - 2 - 3

HE'S A JOLLY GOOD FELLOW

England

NOTES ON THE FOURTH STRING

Practice each exercise carefully. Remember to keep your fingers arched over the strings.

PICKUP NOTES

Music doesn't always begin on beat one. When you begin after beat one, the notes before the first full measure are called **pickup notes**. Following are two examples of pickup notes. Count the missing beats out loud before you begin playing.

When a song begins with pickup notes, the last measure will be short the exact number of beats used as pickups.

WORRIED MAN BLUES

Traditional

PLAYING CHORDS

A **chord** is sounded when more than two notes or strings are played at the same time. To begin you will be playing chords on three strings with only one finger depressed. Disregard the light gray finger numbers on strings 4, 5, and 6 until you can easily play the one-finger versions of the chords below.

The C Chord

The G7 Chord

Study the illustrations for the chords above. An "o" above a string indicates that the string should be played "open" (not depressed by a finger). An "x" above a string indicates that the string should not be strummed. Refer to the hand positions in the photos below for additional visual guidance.

Depress the strings indicated with the tips of your fingers. Arch your fingers to avoid touching strings that are to be played open. Strum over the strings with a downward motion. All strings should sound as one, not separately.

Practice the following exercise strumming once for each slash mark. Keep a steady beat, and change chord fingerings quickly.

Now apply this strum to the song below.

TOM DOOLEY

Traditional

Next, let's try two more chords: G and D7. Notice that the G chord can be played two different ways.

The G Chord

The G Chord
(alternative fingering)

The D7 Chord

Strum once for each slash mark below.

G   D 7

35

G   D 7   G   D 7   G

Review the fingering for the C chord and then practice Exercise 36 until you can play it well. Whenever you are moving between the C chord and the D7 chord, keep the first finger down.

G   C   D 7   G

36

PAY ME MY MONEY DOWN

Georgia Sea Islands

G   D 7

37

Pay me, oh pay me, pay me my mon - ey down.

G

Pay me or go to jail, pay me my mon - ey down.

The following exercises use the four chords you have learned so far. The chords are arranged in sequences called **chord progressions**.

MOVING FROM CHORD TO CHORD

As you are playing one chord, look ahead to the next and get your fingers in position. Then, switch chords using a minimum of hand motion.

Trade off strumming the chords and playing the melody with your teacher or a friend.

12-BAR ROCK

You can also play the G, C, and D7 chords with "Worried Man Blues" on page 16.

TIES

A curved line which connects two notes of the same pitch is called a **tie**. The first note is struck and held for the value of both notes. The second note should not be played again. Look at the following example of tied notes.

42

1 - 2 - 3 - 4 - 1   2   3 - 4 - 1 - 2   3   4 - 1   2 - 3 - 4

5 BEATS   **4 BEATS**   **2 BEATS**

Practice trading off on melody and chords in these pieces.

AMAZING GRACE

Traditional

43

A - maz - ing   grace,   how   sweet   the   sound   that

1 - 2 - 3 - 1 - 2

saved   a   wretch   like   me. _____   I   once   was   lost,   but

1 - 2 - 3 - 1 - 2

now   am   found;   was   blind,   but   now   I   see. _____

RIFFIN'

44

WHEN THE SAINTS GO MARCHING IN

Traditional

G

(1) 2 3 4   1 - 2 - 3 - 4 - 1   2   3   4   1 - 2 - 3 - 4 - 1   2   3   4
Oh when the   saints _____   go march-ing   in _____   oh when the

D7   **G**

1 - 2 - 3 - 4 - 1 - 2 - 3   4   1 - 2 - 3 - 4 -
saints   go   march - ing   in _____   Lord, I   want   to

C   **G**   **D7 G**

1   2 - 3 - 4 - 1 - 2 - 3   4   1 - 2 - 3 - 4 - 1
be   in that num-ber _____   when the saints   go   march - ing   in. _____

WILL THE CIRCLE BE UNBORKEN

Country Gospel

G

Will   the   cir - cle _____   be un - bro - ken, _____   by   and

C   **G**

by,   Lord,   by   and   by? _____   There's   a

bet - ter _____   home   a - wait - ing, _____   in   the

D7   **G**

sky,   Lord, _____   in   the _____   sky. _____

21

NOTES ON THE FIFTH STRING

A — OPEN — Ledger lines

B — 2nd FRET / 2nd FINGER

C — 3rd FRET / 3rd FINGER

47

Hold 2nd finger down _

BLUES BASS

48

A

D 7   A

E 7   D 7   A

Practice these familiar melodies until you feel comfortable playing them. Remember to look ahead as you play so you can prepare for the next notes.

JOSHUA FOUGHT THE BATTLE OF JERICHO

Spiritual

GREENSLEEVES

England

NOTES ON THE SIXTH STRING

E   F   G

OPEN

OPEN   1st FRET   3rd FRET
                     1st FINGER   3rd FINGER

E   F   G

After you play these exercises, write the letter names below each note.

51

Hold 1st finger down

52

53

DOO-WOP

GIVE MY REGARDS TO BROADWAY

George M. Cohan

BASS ROCK

HALF AND WHOLE STEPS

The distance between music tones is measured by half steps and whole steps. On your guitar the distance between one fret and the next fret is a half step. The distance from one fret to the third fret in either direction is called a whole step.

F-SHARP (F#)

When a **sharp** (#) is placed in front of a note, the note is raised a half step and played one fret higher. A sharp placed before a note affects all notes on the same line or space that follow in that measure. Following are the three F#s that appear on the fretboard to the right:

3 F#s

1st STRING
2nd FRET   **4th STRING**
              4th FRET   **6th STRING**
                            2nd FRET

Practice each of these finger exercises many times.

DANNY BOY (LONDONDERRY AIR)

Ireland

26

KEY SIGNATURES

Instead of writing a sharp sign before every F in a song, one sharp is placed at the beginning of the line. This is called a **key signature** and indicates that every F in the song should be played as F♯. In "Shenandoah" there will be an arrow above each F♯ to remind you to play F♯.

SHENANDOAH

Sea Shanty

Oh Shen - an - doah _____ I long to see you, _____ A -
way _____ you roll-ing riv - er, _____ Oh Shen - an - doah _____
_____ I long to see you, _____ A - way _____ we're bound a -
way _____ a - cross the wide Miss - ou - ri.

SPY RIFF

RESTS

Musical **rests** are moments of silence in music. Each type of note has a matching rest which has the same name and receives the same number of counts.

Whole	Half	Quarter
4 beats	2 beats	1 beat

A rest often requires that you stop the sound of your guitar strings with your right hand as is shown in the photo to the right. This process is called **dampening** the strings. Use the edge of your right palm to touch the strings, and work for little unnecessary movement.

As you play the following exercises that contain both notes and rests, count aloud using numbers for the notes and say the word, "rest," for each beat of silence.

COUNT: 1   2   3 Rest   1 Rest 3 Rest   Rest 2   3   4   1 - 2   Rest Rest

The letter **R** is used in place of the word "rest."

1   2   R   R   R   2   3   4   R   R   R   R   1   R   3   4   1 - 2 - 3   R

DEEP BLUE

RED RIVER VALLEY

Cowboy Song

64

Come and sit by my side if you love me.

Do not has - ten to bid me a - dieu.

But re - mem - ber the Red Riv - er Val - ley,

and the cow - boy who loved you so true. _____

TWANG

65

In $\frac{3}{4}$ a complete measure of rest (3 counts) is written as a whole rest (▬).

ROCK 'N' REST

66

EIGHTH NOTES

An **eighth note** is half the length of a quarter note and receives half a beat in ¼ or ¾ meter.

One eighth note is written with a flag. Consecutive eighth notes are connected with a beam.

To count eighth notes, divide the beat into two, and use "and" between the beats. Count the measure to the right aloud while tapping your foot on the beat.

Eighth notes are played with a **downstroke** (⊓) of the pick on the beat and an **upstroke** (∨) on the "and." This is called **alternate picking**.

Playing the following exercise using alternate picking for all eighth notes and strictly downstrokes for all quarter notes. Practice slowly and steadily at first; then gradually increase the speed.

A double bar with two dots (:||) is a **repeat sign**, and it tells you to play the music a second time.

SEA SHANTY

69

FRÉRE JACQUES

France

70

Fré - re   Jac - ques,   Fré - re   Jac - ques,   dor - mez vous?   Dor - mez vous?
Are you sleep - ing?   Are you sleep - ing?   Broth - er   John,   Broth - er   John,

Son - nez les ma - tin - es,   son - nez les ma - tin - es,   din, din, don;   din, din, don.
Morn-ing bells are ring-ing,   morn-ing bells are ring-ing,   ding, dong, ding;   ding, dong, ding.

SNAKE CHARMER

71

Try playing "Snake Charmer" again, this time on the higher strings. Begin an octave higher with the A note on the second fret of the third string, and use your ear as a guide.

THE STAR-SPANGLED BANNER

Key/Smith

MORE STRUMMING

The alternating down-up stroke pattern you have already played on eighth notes can also be applied to strumming. As you practice the following exercise, keep you wrist relaxed and flexible. The down-up motion will be much faster and easier if you use motion of the wrist only, rather than of the entire arm. This wrist motion feels a little like shaking water off the hand.

BASIC DOWN-UP STRUM

STRUM VARIATIONS

A variation of the basic down-up strum misses the upstroke or "and" of the first beat. Remember to keep the down-up motion going and miss the strings on the "and" of beat one.

This variation misses two upstrokes. Continue to strum but miss the strings on the "and" of beats one and three.

THE Em CHORD

Em

The E minor chord is one of the easiest chords on the guitar. Arch your fingers and play on the tips to avoid touching the other open strings.

76

HEY, HO, NOBODY HOME

England

77

Hey,   ho,   no - bod - y home.   Meat, nor drink, nor

mon - ey have I none,   yet will I be mer - ry.   (ry.)

SHALOM CHAVERIM
(Peace, My Friend)

Israel

78

Sha - lom, cha - ve - rim! Sha - lom, cha - ve - rim! Sha - lom,   sha -

lom! Le - hit - ra - ot, le - hit - ra - ot. Sha - lom,   sha - lom.

CHORD PAIRS

As you move between different chords, if one or more fingers remain on the same note, allow them to stay pressed as you switch chords. In the following progression there is a common finger between the G and Em chords and a common finger btween the C and D7 chords.

Practice the following chord progressions until you can play them steadily and without any hesitation between chord changes. Try to move your fingers to a new chord as a unit instead of "letting your fingers do the walking" one at a time.

You can vary the strumming by alternating between a bass note (usually the lowest note of a chord and the name of the chord) and the remainder of the chord. This style of accompaniment is referred to as the **bass note strum**, or "boom chick" rhythm.

THE D CHORD

D

84   Em   D   C   D

85   Em   D   C   Em   D   C

THIS TRAIN

African American

86   **G**

This train   is   bound for   glo - ry,   this train. ____

D

This train   is   bound for   glo - ry,   this train. ____

G   **G7**   **C**   **G**   **D**

This train   is   bound for   glo - ry,   if   you   want to   ride it   you   must be ho - ly.

G   **D**   **G**

This train   is   bound for   glo - ry,   this train. ____

BOOGIE BASS

The next example uses a variation on the bass note strum technique. This time, strike the bass note and then strum the remainder of the chord twice.

On "Simple Gifts" you can play the melody (Part 1), the harmony line (Part 2), or the chordal accompaniment.

Practice these strums before playing "Simple Gifts."

SIMPLE GIFTS

Shaker Song

C-SHARP (C#)

C#

C#

2nd STRING
2nd FRET
2nd FINGER

ROCKIN' BLUES

THE A7 CHORD

95

96

DOWN IN THE VALLEY

Traditional

97

Down in the val - ley, val - ley so
Hear the wind blow, dear, hear the wind

low, _____ } hang your head o -
blow, _____

ver, hear the wind blow. _____

41

MINUET IN G

J.S. BACH

98

Repeat to top of page

TIME IS ON MY SIDE

Jerry Ragovoy

GRAND FINALE

CHORD CHART

In this chart you will find the chords learned in this book as well as several other common chords you may see in music you are playing.

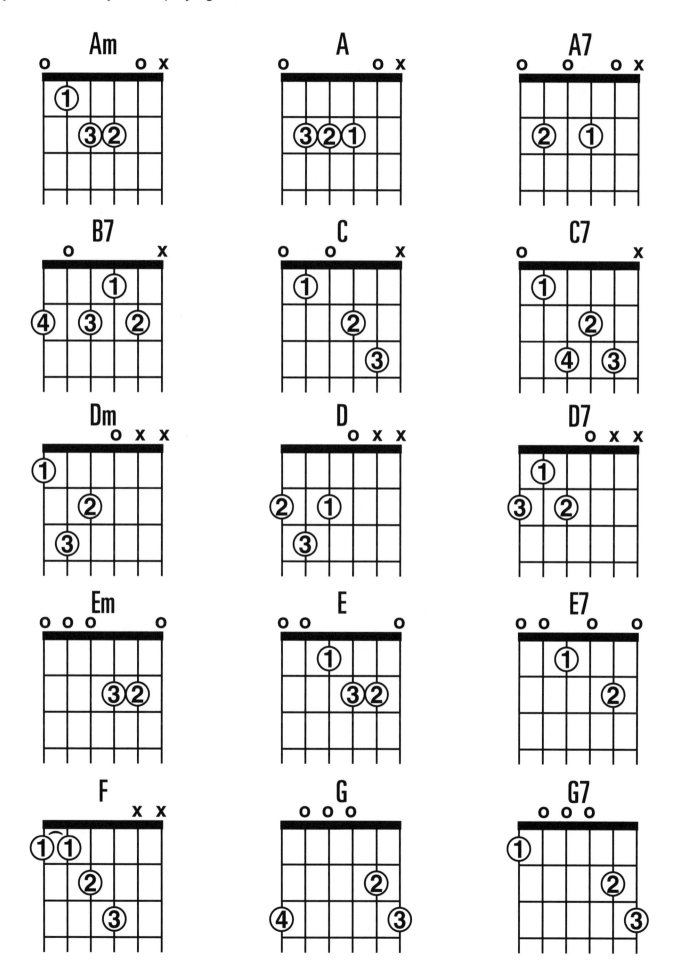

HAL LEONARD GUITAR METHOD

METHOD BOOKS, SONGBOOKS AND REFERENCE BOOKS

THE HAL LEONARD GUITAR METHOD is designed for anyone just learning to play acoustic or electric guitar. It is based on years of teaching guitar students of all ages, and it also reflects some of the best guitar teaching ideas from around the world. This comprehensive method includes: A learning sequence carefully paced with clear instructions; popular songs which increase the incentive to learn to play; versatility – can be used as self-instruction or with a teacher; audio accompaniments so that students have fun and sound great while practicing.

BOOK 1
00699010	Book Only	$8.99
00699027	Book/Online Audio	$12.99
00697341	Book/Online Audio + DVD	$24.99
00697318	DVD Only	$19.99
00155480	Deluxe Beginner Edition (Book, CD, DVD, Online Audio/ Video & Chord Poster)	$19.99

COMPLETE (BOOKS 1, 2 & 3)
00699040	Book Only	$16.99
00697342	Book/Online Audio	$24.99

BOOK 2
00699020	Book Only	$8.99
00697313	Book/Online Audio	$12.99

BOOK 3
00699030	Book Only	$8.99
00697316	Book/Online Audio	$12.99

Prices, contents and availability subject to change without notice.

STYLISTIC METHODS

ACOUSTIC GUITAR
00697347	Method Book/Online Audio	$17.99
00237969	Songbook/Online Audio	$16.99

BLUEGRASS GUITAR
00697405	Method Book/Online Audio	$16.99

BLUES GUITAR
00697326	Method Book/Online Audio (9" x 12")	$16.99
00697344	Method Book/Online Audio (6" x 9")	$15.99
00697385	Songbook/Online Audio (9" x 12")	$14.99
00248636	Kids Method Book/Online Audio	$12.99

BRAZILIAN GUITAR
00697415	Method Book/Online Audio	$17.99

CHRISTIAN GUITAR
00695947	Method Book/Online Audio	$16.99
00697408	Songbook/CD Pack	$14.99

CLASSICAL GUITAR
00697376	Method Book/Online Audio	$15.99

COUNTRY GUITAR
00697337	Method Book/Online Audio	$22.99
00697400	Songbook/Online Audio	$19.99

FINGERSTYLE GUITAR
00697378	Method Book/Online Audio	$21.99
00697432	Songbook/Online Audio	$16.99

FLAMENCO GUITAR
00697363	Method Book/Online Audio	$15.99

FOLK GUITAR
00697414	Method Book/Online Audio	$16.99

JAZZ GUITAR
00695359	Book/Online Audio	$22.99
00697386	Songbook/Online Audio	$15.99

JAZZ-ROCK FUSION
00697387	Book/Online Audio	$24.99

R&B GUITAR
00697356	Book/Online Audio	$19.99
00697433	Songbook/CD Pack	$14.99

ROCK GUITAR
00697319	Book/Online Audio	$16.99
00697383	Songbook/Online Audio	$16.99

ROCKABILLY GUITAR
00697407	Book/Online Audio	$16.99

OTHER METHOD BOOKS

BARITONE GUITAR METHOD
00242055	Book/Online Audio	$12.99

GUITAR FOR KIDS
00865003	Method Book 1/Online Audio	$12.99
00697402	Songbook/Online Audio	$9.99
00128437	Method Book 2/Online Audio	$12.99

MUSIC THEORY FOR GUITARISTS
00695790	Book/Online Audio	$19.99

TENOR GUITAR METHOD
00148330	Book/Online Audio	$12.99

12-STRING GUITAR METHOD
00249528	Book/Online Audio	$19.99

METHOD SUPPLEMENTS

ARPEGGIO FINDER
00697352	6" x 9" Edition	$6.99
00697351	9" x 12" Edition	$9.99

BARRE CHORDS
00697406	Book/Online Audio	$14.99

CHORD, SCALE & ARPEGGIO FINDER
00697410	Book Only	$19.99

GUITAR TECHNIQUES
00697389	Book/Online Audio	$16.99

INCREDIBLE CHORD FINDER
00697200	6" x 9" Edition	$7.99
00697208	9" x 12" Edition	$7.99

INCREDIBLE SCALE FINDER
00695568	6" x 9" Edition	$9.99
00695490	9" x 12" Edition	$9.99

LEAD LICKS
00697345	Book/Online Audio	$10.99

RHYTHM RIFFS
00697346	Book/Online Audio	$14.99

SONGBOOKS

CLASSICAL GUITAR PIECES
00697388	Book/Online Audio	$9.99

EASY POP MELODIES
00697281	Book Only	$7.99
00697440	Book/Online Audio	$14.99

(MORE) EASY POP MELODIES
00697280	Book Only	$6.99
00697269	Book/Online Audio	$14.99

(EVEN MORE) EASY POP MELODIES
00699154	Book Only	$6.99
00697439	Book/Online Audio	$14.99

EASY POP RHYTHMS
00697336	Book Only	$7.99
00697441	Book/Online Audio	$14.99

(MORE) EASY POP RHYTHMS
00697338	Book Only	$7.99
00697322	Book/Online Audio	$14.99

(EVEN MORE) EASY POP RHYTHMS
00697340	Book Only	$7.99
00697323	Book/Online Audio	$14.99

EASY POP CHRISTMAS MELODIES
00697417	Book Only	$9.99
00697416	Book/Online Audio	$14.99

EASY POP CHRISTMAS RHYTHMS
00278177	Book Only	$6.99
00278175	Book/Online Audio	$14.99

EASY SOLO GUITAR PIECES
00110407	Book Only	$9.99

REFERENCE

GUITAR PRACTICE PLANNER
00697401	Book Only	$5.99

GUITAR SETUP & MAINTENANCE
00697427	6" x 9" Edition	$14.99
00697421	9" x 12" Edition	$12.99

For more info, songlists, or to purchase these and more books from your favorite music retailer, go to

halleonard.com

HAL•LEONARD®